I Do On Purpose

Planning a Wedding with Intention

(Without Losing Your Mind)

Kaci Willwerth

Copyright © 2026 Kaci Willwerth

All rights reserved. This book or any parts may not be reproduced in any form, electronic, mechanical, photocopy or otherwise, without written permission from the author. For permission requests, write to the publisher, addressed "Attention:

Permissions Coordinator," at the address below.
Owl Publishing, LLC.
www.owlpublishinghouse.com

ISBN: 979-8-234-04581-2 (paperback)
979-8-234-04582-9 (hardcover)

Library of Congress Control Number: In Process

Praise for *I Do on Purpose*

"Kaci Willwerth has spent almost two decades shaping the wedding and events industry with her expertise, heart, and leadership. Few professionals bring the level of insight and authenticity that she does, and this book is a natural extension of that work. It's a thoughtful, experience-driven guide that keeps the focus where it belongs—on meaning, intention, and celebration. A must-read from a true industry leader. Bravo, Kaci."

~ **David Everett,** Award-**winning** Event Designer

"Kaci approaches her work as a wedding planner with intention, elegance, and a steady, confident calm that immediately puts her clients at ease. Her thoughtful leadership and refined attention to detail create space for creativity to flourish and teams to work in seamless harmony. As a fellow seasoned wedding professional, I have long admired her ability to bring people together with clarity, grace, and genuine care. This book is a beautiful reflection of the heart, purpose, and quiet passion she brings to every celebration she touches."

~ **Alexander Johnnides**, Owner & Lead Photographer, Longbrook Photography

"Kaci Willwerth has coordinated hundreds of weddings at our venue and possesses all the qualities of an exceptional and well connected wedding planner! She always arrives prepared, calm and is highly communicative to execute seamless events. Kaci is quite an energetic and trustworthy team player with a bubbly, personable demeanor. She is a dynamo planner who makes all the wedding day tasks look effortless for her couples and the vendors."

~ **Kelly Dantinne,** Venue Proprietor of Excelsior, Lancaster, PA

"Kaci has written a book that honestly explores the ups, downs, and reality of wedding planning. Even though things rarely go exactly as planned, that unpredictability is part of the joy. This book will help you understand what truly goes into planning your big day while easing your mind about the inevitable stresses along the way. I have been in the industry for over 25 years and have had the pleasure of working alongside Kaci for many of them. She is deeply knowledgeable and genuinely caring with her clients, combining compassion with the get-er-done attitude required for real success."

~ **Tara L Folker,** Owner & Designer, Splints & Daisies

"As an owner of an event entertainment company, I truly appreciate Kaci's insight and knowledge that she has shared in this book. I've had the pleasure of knowing Kaci and working with her for many years. Her cool, calm and collected nature has allowed her to be someone you can put faith in and trust that every detail of an event is being taken care of. She truly loves what she does and it shows. Being a fellow wedding vendor, I appreciate how she not only relates to those planning a wedding, but also to the vendors who are working together to make the day a success. She understands every angle of planning a wedding day, but throughout the book she keeps it very simple and offers stress-free ways for couples to plan each step of the way. Most importantly - the book is a great reminder of what the end result should be. It's not in the details, but rather the love and new journey that couples will share after they say "I Do."

~ **Eddie Ward, Professional** DJ, Owner, Cutting Edge Productions

"Having worked alongside Kaci at our wedding venue, Bluestone Estate, over the past nine years, I found this book to be more than a wedding guide. It treats planning as a meaningful first step into marriage. It reminds couples to choose connection over appearances and presence over pressure. It is a heartfelt nudge to be fully present on your wedding day, drink it in, and walk into marriage with purpose and grace."

~ **Erin Vinelli, Venue** Owner of Bluestone Estate

Dedication

to my mother, Candi, and to my husband, Jared,
and my kids, Kloie and Kash

Contents

Introduction

Congratulations! You're engaged! There's probably a ring on your finger, champagne in the fridge and a Pinterest board that's already spiraling out of control. Welcome to wedding planning – a beautiful, chaotic adventure where you'll discover things about yourself, your partner and your level of patience that you never knew existed.

Before you dive into budgets, bouquets, and battles over the guest list, take a deep breath. This book isn't here to make you feel behind schedule, overwhelmed, or give you massive checklists to lose sleep over. This is your guide to planning a wedding that's meaningful, memorable and a reflection of *you.*

I have been a wedding planner for most of my adult life, and I've seen couples get lost in the stress instead of the excitement. When I received a 3:30am text from one of my brides saying "I can't sleep", I knew it was time to write a book that kept the purpose (and the humor) of weddings in focus. I have witnessed couples turning something beautiful into a full-time stress job over and over again. Being more intentional about your wedding starts with laughing more and panicking less. This isn't your typical "wedding planning to-do list" that is 500 pages long. I wanted to write a book that wasn't overwhelming, full of checklists, and that summarizes the most important details for such a special day. This is your honest, witty companion for planning a wedding that feels like *you* – not an overwhelming Pinterest board come to life.

You won't find perfection here. You'll find real talk, useful advice and reminders that your wedding is not a performance; it's a celebration. A celebration of you and your partner, your love, and your future life together. Think of me as your brutally honest maid of honor; the one that tells you the truth while keeping the champagne flowing. By the end of the book, you will know how to handle budgets, hire your vendor team and how to handle your opinionated parents or future in-laws with grace (or at least with a decent fake smile). You will know how to plan with purpose, not pressure, and will be reminded that your wedding is one incredible day in an even more incredible story.

So, grab a glass of tea or tequila (no judgement), put your feet up, and let's plan a wedding that feels intentional and feels like *you.*

Ready? Let's do it.

CHAPTER 1

The Why Before the White Dress

Find Your Why Before You Say "I Do" to Anything

Picture this: You just got engaged. You're staring at your brand-new sparkly ring, taking ring selfies, feeling all the happy emotions: love, excitement, and maybe mild panic, when suddenly someone asks, *"So…when is the big day?"*

This question is the wedding equivalent of asking a college freshman about their five-year career plan. You're still figuring out how to call each other "fiancé" without sounding like you're ordering something off a pretentious French menu.

Before you pick a dress, choose a color palette or ask your cousin who once took a photography class to *"just do the pictures,"* you need to know **why** you're doing this.

And no, "because I'm in love" or "because they're cute" isn't enough. Love is the foundation, yes. But so is concrete and I know you wouldn't build your dream home without a blueprint.

Your **why** is that blueprint.

If your purpose is "to celebrate with the people we love most" or "to create a day that reflects our love story and the life we're building together," that purpose becomes the compass that will guide every decision about your wedding. Without it, wedding planning turns into a frantic Pinterest scavenger hunt where the prize is…burnout.

Your ***wedding why*** is the heartbeat of the day. It's the North Star. The foundation. The reason you're gathering everyone you know and love, dressing them up and feeding them an expensive meal. ***Here's the truth most people skip:*** If you don't start with your purpose, you'll end up planning a wedding that feels like it belongs to a fictional character in a book called "Bridal Expectations" instead of you.

Some couples want a giant celebration. Some want an intimate moment. Some want a party that feels like a warm hug, while others want a rager that feels like Vegas but with better lighting. Whatever it is, your why shapes every decision you make. Without it? You'll be tossed around by trends, opinions, and every vendor who swears you *simply must have* a champagne tower pour or a cupcake tower (beautiful, yes; essential, no).

But clarity on your why only works if you and your fiancé both share it.

The Joint Vision Exercise

This exercise is designed to get the conversation started between you and your future spouse. Sit down together, pour a drink, and answer a few simple but powerful questions separately. Take your time and be completely honest.

Joint Vision exercise

1. **What do I want our guests to remember most about our wedding?**

    Example: that it was really fun, heartfelt and no one went home hungry.

    Example: that it was a reflection of your personalities.

    Example: our creative signature cocktails and delicious dinner.

2. **What do I want to feel most on our wedding day?**

    Example: present, connected and not worried about all of the little details.

    Example: fun, relaxed and stress-free

    Example: the dance floor and photo booth were packed all night long.

3. **What matters more: the experience or the aesthetics?**

Hot tip: *Saying "both" is a trap. Pick your lane and stay sane.*

Example: The experience - it was a relaxed, smooth and fun day.

Example: The experience - cocktail hour was so fun and dinner felt intimate.

Example: The aesthetics - the centerpieces and tablescapes were stunning.

Example: The aesthetics - the venue was unique and set the tone.

Joint Vision exercise

4. **What do I not care about at all?**

   Example: Favors, elaborate cake toppers or the seating chart being an elaborate display that people glance at until they find their name.

   Example: The size of the bridesmaids bouquets, wine service during dinner or cocktail napkins with your pet's face on them that people throw away.

   Example: If you have 5 or 6 passed hors d' oeuvres, if you have green beans or asparagus as a side or adding the seafood station for an extra $20 per person.

Once you complete these charts independently, compare your list with your partner's. What do you agree on? Does anyone have a non-negotiable? Use this exercise as a chance to have a conversation about your expectations and dreams. After you finish this exercise you will most likely feel refreshed and excited to start planning your special day together and on the same page.

You might be perfectly aligned…or you might be staring at each other blankly thinking, "Huh. Interesting." Either way, this conversation will save you hours of indecision later. These lists will help you better understand each other and keep each other focused on what is most important to you as you make one decision after another…after another. It will also help steer the opinionated family members (See *"How To Say No"* in

Chapter 2) towards your vision and priorities. Keep these lists close to you, make copies, put them on the fridge, in your wedding planning binder, and in your memory. Let it be your North Star every time someone tries to sell you on a dove release, a sprig of sage on each place setting or something that isn't important or meaningful to you. I assure you that you will need to remind yourself of your why and what's most important to you very often during the planning process.

Finding your wedding why won't tell you what color linens to choose, but it *will* save you from losing your mind over them. It's the reason you can say yes with confidence, no without guilt and "we're skipping that" without explaining yourself. Your why is the soul of your celebration, the part that doesn't need a filter or a hashtag.

So, plan the party, pop the champagne and enjoy every minute, but never forget why you showed up in the first place. That's the part that actually lasts.

CHAPTER 2

Guest Lists: Hunger Games Edition

Welcome to the single most emotional spreadsheet you will ever create. Guest list planning sounds simple, right? Just make a list of the people you love…right? Wrong. It's like deciding who gets a seat on a lifeboat…except the Titanic in this scenario is your catering budget, and your aunt is suggesting you "just make room" for her neighbor that you've only met once in your life. This is where you get your first taste of The Great Wedding Debate. Your purpose will help you here, because if you're focused on meaning, you'll invite the people who genuinely support your marriage, not just eat your hors d'oeuvres. If you haven't spoken to them in fifteen years, they probably don't need filet mignon and an open bar for 5 hours on your dime.

Here's a 5-step guide to help you with family expectations without having to act like Katniss Everdeen and President Snow in The Hunger Games. Start by setting your magic number, then identify your must-have guests, tackle plus-ones and kids, and finally, make your cuts.

5 Easy Steps to Creating Your Guest List

Step 1 The Magic Number

Before you even think about who, figure out **how many**. Your guest count drives your costs more than any other factor. The difference between 100 guests and 150 guests could easily be the price of your honeymoon…or your honeymoon **AND** next year's vacation.

1. Determine your catering budget *(more guidance in Chapter 3)*.

2. Divide your catering budget by the per person cost.

3. That's your cap on your guest list. Period. Take the emotions out and remember: simple math will save you future tears and sleepless nights.

Step 2 The Inner Circle Rule

Your wedding day should be filled with people who:

1. You genuinely want to be there.
2. Know and support your relationship.
3. You'd be okay having in your "life highlight reel" forever.

If they haven't met your partner, don't know your last name or will need to ask a stranger at their table, "So, how do you know the bride?" they're probably not your inner circle.

Step 3 Plus Ones - The Diplomacy Game

Plus-ones can turn a 120-person wedding into a 150-person wedding faster than you can say "seating chart." A plus-one isn't just a chair - it's a meal, a drink (or 4), a favor, a slice of cake, and possibly a stranger lingering in your wedding photos forever. Be intentional. Your wedding is not a networking event or a first date experiment. Invite people you know, love, and would happily take out dinner on a regular Wednesday evening. Everyone else can sit this one out.

If they are married, engaged or long-term cohabiting, then invite the partner. Serious, stable relationships you know about? Invite the partner. Random Tinder date of the week? Hard pass.

When in doubt, make a blanket rule and stick to it. People respect consistency (or at least stop complaining once they realize you're not making exceptions).

Step 4 Kids - Yes or No?

This is one of the biggest drama points in guest list history that could break up an entire family. I wish I was joking.

If you want a child-free wedding say it kindly, but clearly on the invitation. Offer resources for childcare nearby. Stand firm – once you make one exception, it's a slippery slope to a toddler mosh pit on the dance floor and near your very fragile centerpieces.

If you're including kids expect to adjust your schedule (and maybe your candles in glass hurricane vases down the aisle). Consider a kids' table with activities so they're happy and the parents can relax.

Step 5 **The Cut List**

Sometimes the list, even when following these steps, gets unwieldy. The number of plus ones and cousins has exceeded your budget or venue capacity, and you need to make some tough decisions. Here's a trick to trim down the guest list and minimize any guilty feelings.

1. First, take the list and make a "must invite" list.
2. Then, make a "would be nice" list.
3. Start with list 1 and then determine how many of group 2 you can add based on budget and capacity.

In trimming down your **"must invite"** ask yourself:

- Have we spoken in the last year?
- Would I be genuinely sad if they weren't there?
- Are we inviting them because we want them there or because someone else told us to invite them?

Let's be clear, your guest list is not a suggestion box; it's the Hunger Games. There will be tears, dramatic conversations and at least one person who genuinely thought their plus-one was guaranteed to be invited. Only those who have shown up for your life, your love and your marriage earn a seat at the table. Understand that people might be frustrated and maybe even hurt that they weren't included, but appeasing everyone else can't be your guiding light. Remember, it's your wedding. Your guest list should reflect your relationships, not your obligation or a quota. The more intentional you are now, the less likely you'll be hiding in the bathroom from your fourth cousin Eddie halfway through the reception. May your boundaries be strong, your tables full and the odds ever in your favor.

CHAPTER 3

How to Say No

(Without Starting Family Drama)

Once you know your purpose and create your guest list, you'll also know when to politely, but firmly, say "no." It's crucial to get comfortable with saying "no" early on in wedding planning. By the time wedding day arrives, it just might be your favorite word. It's important because if you say "yes" to almost everything people request and want to be a people pleaser, suddenly you will find yourself saying "yes" to fourteen things you never wanted and at least three of them you don't even remember.

At some point in wedding planning opinions will appear uninvited, like distant cousins for plus-ones you've never met. Everyone suddenly becomes an expert on flowers, food, fonts and why their wedding from 1998 is still the gold standard. Here's the truth no one tells you early enough - not every opinion deserves a response, consideration or an emotional processing session. You are planning a wedding, not hosting a town hall. The goal is not to make everyone happy, the goal is to get married without losing your mind or your vision in the process.

You can say no without being rude or dramatic. You can say it in a way that doesn't scream "I'm about to throw this seating chart out of the window." Start by practicing saying "no" gracefully, confidently and with boundaries so gentle they practically smell like lavender. Wedding planning is not a group project despite what your extended family, co-workers, and that one bridesmaid with excessive opinions might think. Saying "no" is not negative. Saying "no" is self-care with a backbone and zero burnout.

Politely saying no is an art form and luckily, it requires far fewer words than you think. Phrases like "that's not the direction we're going but thank you" or "we've already made a decision and feel really good about it" are the bridal equivalent of a velvet rope. They're kind, clear, and leave no room for follow up questions disguised as concern. You don't owe explanations, spreadsheets or a PowerPoint presentation defending your choices. "No" can be warm, confident and complete - just like your bar menu.

Remember this - every time you say yes to an opinion you don't actually want, you're saying no to your own priorities. Boundaries aren't rude; they're responsible. They protect your budget, your peace, and your partnership, which, *spoiler alert* matter more than whether Aunt Sandy likes the round tables you already reserved. Practice saying no now, because marriage will offer plenty of opportunities to keep using that muscle. Do it with grace, humor, and a smile, and then move on to the things that truly deserve your energy, like cake tasting and forever.

Saying no is about setting boundaries and protecting your peace. Again, let's keep remembering that this is *your* wedding and it should be a reflection of you in every aspect.

Practice Saying No!

Request

Your cousin wants to bring a boyfriend she met last Tuesday.

Response

"Right now, we're keeping the guest list to people we know personally. We're not able to offer plus-ones across the board, but we're so excited to celebrate with you there!"

Suggestion

A relative wants you to add a prayer, readings and/or a unity candle.

Response

"We are keeping the ceremony light and simple, so we aren't adding any extra elements, but thank you for the suggestion!"

Suggestion

Aunt Linda says "You *have* to have a receiving line. It's tradition."

Response

"We're actually going to skip that so we can spend more time with our guests during the cocktail hour, but we can't wait to hug you then!"

Suggestion

Your co-worker insists that you play the hype song that you both listen to at work for your Wedding Party Introductions.

Response

"We actually already have a plan with our DJ, but thank you for thinking of us. We can't wait to see you on the dance floor!"

Request

"Can I bring my toddler? She loves weddings!"

Response

"We're keeping the wedding to adults only, so parents can relax and enjoy the night. Thanks for understanding!"

The trick is gratitude + redirection. You acknowledge the suggestion, thank them and then steer them toward your vision. Don't forget to remind them how excited you are to celebrate with them. Works like a charm – and keeps you on purpose!

CHAPTER 4

The Budget Without the Panic

The Budget Fairy Tale

Somewhere out there, there's a bride who planned her dream wedding, stayed on budget and had no drama. She lives in a cottage with a talking deer and bakes cookies for a living. No one has ever met her.

That said, you want to budget like a boss and not a Bridezilla so you don't end up eating ramen for the next three years because of how much you paid for your wedding. A wedding budget is important and isn't about killing the fun – it's about making sure your spending actually matches what matters most to you. Think of it like building a playlist: you want every dollar to hit the right note, not just fill space. A budget is your secret weapon for creating the wedding you actually want without going broke.

On the next page, I'll break down the five steps that I've found most helpful for couples struggling to make sense of their budget and help you prioritize what's most important to you.

Step 1 **What's a Realistic Number?**

Start with a total amount that you're willing (and able) to spend. This is not the "Pinterest dream" number. This is the **real-life, won't-send-you-into-credit-card-therapy** number.

Your budget is the spine of your wedding. Not the venue, not the dress, not even the photographer. The budget is the only thing silently keeping the entire operation from falling apart like a poorly assembled charcuterie board. It's not about money; it's about values. It's about deciding, as a team, what matters most. Do you want stunning photography that you'll cherish forever? Or do you want a champagne tower? Do you want a string quartet? It's not just numbers – it's alignment, intention and the priceless gift of not entering marriage with the financial equivalent of a hangover.

If you're getting financial help from family, have the conversation early. Yes, it might be awkward. But it's a lot less awkward than assuming your parents are covering the open bar only to find out they meant "open…to the idea of guests buying their own drinks." If your family has offered to help with the wedding, communicate clearly on what they are offering. Are they giving you one lump sum for you to spend on what you want? Or are they offering to pay for specific items such as the flowers and band? You need to know this upfront so it doesn't get messy and dramatic down the road.

Step 2 Choose Categories and Prioritize

Break your budget into categories **based on your priorities**, not tradition.

If you and your partner are foodies, it would make sense that 30% of your budget would go towards catering. If you care more about the dance floor than the flowers, shift the money accordingly. If you truly don't care about favors, skip them entirely. (Newsflash: only your mom and best friend are saving that personalized shot glass.)

Here's a general starting point – tweak as needed based on what's most important to you:

Basic Wedding Categories

Category	Percentage
Venue	37%
Catering	28%
Wedding Planner	6%
Photography/Videography	7-8%
Music/Entertainment	8-10%
Flowers & Décor	8-10%
Attire & Beauty	5-8%
Alcohol	8%
Officiant	1%
Cake & Desserts	2%
Everything Else *(stationary, favors, transportation, etc.)*	5-10%

Your categories might be different, and your percentages won't be exactly the same as mine on the previous page. This isn't a rule; it's just a starting point for you to go into negotiations with your vendors with your eyes wide open.

Step 3 Beware of the Budget C.R.E.E.P.

Some costs have a way of sneaking up on you and exploding your budget. What is the budget CREEP?

C.R.E.E.P. = **Couples Rationalizing Every Extra Purchase**

There is a moment in almost every wedding planning process when you look at your spreadsheet and think:

Wait. How did we get here?

You didn't wake up one morning and decide to spend an extra $8,000. It happened slowly. Quietly. Politely. That, my friend, is **Budget C.R.E.E.P.**

It sounds like this:

- "It's only $400 more."
- "We deserve it."
- "It's our day!"
- "Everyone else is doing it."
- "We'll regret it if we don't."

Individually? These statements feel harmless. Collectively? They are financially devastating.

Budget creep doesn't arrive with drama or an outrageous extravagance; it arrives disguised as upgrades. Small, barely-there upgrades. The florist suggests upgraded centerpieces and chargers for only $15 more per guest. The photographer recommends an extra hour for just $500. The venue offers a late-night snack option as low as $8 per person.

"Only" is the most expensive word in wedding planning. Because remember: $15 × 150 guests isn't $15. It's $2,250. That extra hour? Now you need extra DJ time, extra venue time, extra staffing. And suddenly the small decision isn't small anymore. C.R.E.E.P. doesn't explode your budget all at once. It expands it one reasonable sentence at a time.

This certainly does not mean that you forego the extra hour of the photographer, especially when it aligns with your vision for your wedding. You don't need to remove the joy from your wedding; you just need guardrails. Here are some strategies for keeping the creep at bay.

First of all, don't agree to upgrades on the spot. Take time to discuss and see if it matches your budget and expectations. Say: "We'd love to think about that and get back to you." Time cools emotional spending, which can be hard to avoid in the moment. Second, be prepared to bring your calculator. Never agree to "just $12 more per guest" right away. Multiply it immediately to make sure you understand the full impact of that upgrade on your budget, because $12 is much different than $1,200. Always decide based on the full number.

Last, before adding anything, ask: *"Does this deepen the meaning of our day or just increase the price?"* That question alone will save you thousands.

Step 4 — Splurge vs. Save

You don't have to splurge on everything and you definitely don't have to save on everything. Splurge on what matters most to you, save on what doesn't – guilt free.

The magic is knowing where your money actually matters and where you're basically setting cash on fire. Here are some examples of ways that you might decide to save and places where I've found it's worth the extra money.

Splurge

A band that will keep your guests on the dance floor all night.

A photographer whose work you love.

Hair and makeup professionals because this is *not* the day to gamble with humidity and hairspray.

A Wedding Coordinator/Planner so you can enjoy your wedding day instead of managing crises.

Save

Renting simple tablecloths instead of custom embroidered ones that no one will remember.

Buy wedding shoes that don't cost as much as weekend getaway.

Opt for digital RSVPs, and online suites to eliminate postage and stationary costs.

Wedding favors that no one takes home.

Step 5 The Cushion

Always, always, ALWAYS build in a 5-10% buffer for surprise costs because you will have surprise costs and you don't want to be caught without a plan.

These costs can be anything from umbrellas for unexpected rain, to the extra hour you decide to keep the band playing because your guests are having too much fun. If you don't build a cushion, your budget will behave like an elastic waistband and stretch until it suddenly snaps, leaving you without cover. I also refer to a cushion as an "oh no" fund, an "oops" fund or "money we don't talk about unless absolutely necessary." This portion of the budget is used for emergencies, last-minute add-ons, oversights, mistakes, and/or things you swore you wouldn't buy until you realize you absolutely had to. It's not wasted money. It's insurance for your sanity.

It doesn't matter how Type A, color-coded or triple-confirmed your plan is; weddings have a way of surprising unsuspecting couples like it's their side hustle. Things you aren't even thinking about right now might include the delivery fee for the cake or rentals, a cake cutting fee (yes, that's a thing) and the coffee/dessert bar that, surprisingly, isn't included in your catering package.

I can almost guarantee there will be something that you fall in love with late in the game. It might be a second dress for dancing at the reception, a second pair of shoes, a neon sign with your future last name on it, or an upgraded champagne toast. A cushion keeps these budget shocks from turning into full on panic attacks. You'll thank yourself later. And if, for some reason, you don't use this cushion, take it along on your honeymoon or splurge on something fun in your home. There's no downside in preparing for a bit of budget breathing room.

Staying Realistic

Staying realistic about your wedding budget is less about spreadsheets and more about self-awareness. Before you fall in love with a champagne tower, a live painter and a string quartet that only plays Taylor Swift, pause and ask: is this aligned with our real life or just our Pinterest life? A realistic budget honors your priorities without pretending money is Monopoly cash. It acknowledges that "just one upgrade" happens approximately 13 times and that every "small add-on" has a very real price tag. When you decide in advance where you'll splurge, where you'll save and where you'll say a confident *"no thank you,"* your budget stops feeling restrictive and starts feeling intentional - like a plan that lets you celebrate joyfully *and* still afford groceries and a marriage that doesn't begin with financial regret. Refer back to Chapter 4 as often as you need to and remember that your budget is your BFF, not the B word.

CHAPTER 5

Finding The Perfect Venue

Finding your wedding venue is kind of like house hunting, but with more emotions, fewer square feet and significantly more pressure from your mother-in-law. You're not just picking a space – you're choosing the backdrop of your happily ever after photos and the place where your cousin Bob will end up on the dance floor with his tie around his head. Your venue decides a lot more than where you'll say "I do." It influences almost every decision that you make – what you wear, what you eat and how your guests feel (and sweat) because a barn in August with no AC hits different than a ballroom in February. The atmosphere is the first thing your guests will feel and one of the last things they will remember. It sets the stage for the entire day.

The Vision vs. The Budget

Almost every couple starts with a vision: maybe it's a vineyard at sunset, a chic city rooftop or a barn with an outdoor pond. Then reality politely *coughs* and reminds you that vineyards have bugs, rooftops have noise restrictions, and barns aren't always temperature controlled. This moment is like the honeymoon phase of wedding planning wearing off. Suddenly your engaged, selfie-ring-taking smiley fiancé is stressing out more and more at each venue tour. This is also typically when the real opinions from family begin. Your mother loves the vineyard, but your fiancé's mom loves the rooftop. *(Pause and go back to your WHY in Chapter 1. Deep breath. You got this.)*

Your vision for wedding day should be what *you* are picturing when you close your eyes and start to think about your day, not your mother-in-law's vision for hosting her best friends and showing off to her co-workers. Your venue should be a reflection of you and your vision. You should feel at home when you walk in the front door. Choosing your venue is not a compromise like the "what do you want to eat for dinner" conversation. This is your moment to set the stage and to stand up for your vision. It is *your* wedding day. Of course, I understand that family members might be helping support your wedding financially, and these individuals will undoubtedly share their opinion with you.

There might be a moment of "Pick me! Pick me!" This isn't the time to cave on other people's opinions. You haven't even started planning yet. There might be things that you have to compromise on such as a wedding cake instead of an elaborate mini dessert and ice cream bar with more toppings than your local creamery, but the venue should not be one of them. We will discuss how to manage opinions more in Chapter 7.

Don't forget to consider whether your vision is within your budget. Your budget will drive a lot of decisions through the planning process and you have to be realistic about it.

A Few Things To Consider

A 'budget friendly' venue that requires you to rent tables, chairs (and set them up yourself) and electricity may not actually be budget friendly at all. It's budget delusional and will cause you more stress than you may be prepared to handle.

When I hear 'budget friendly' I hear – "you are doing everything yourself and we just unlock the doors for you. Don't forget to take the truck load of trash with you at the end of the night." If you decide to choose such a venue I highly recommend having a small army behind you from a Wedding Planner, delivery crew, set up crew, someone to manage the entire day and a clean-up crew. It's simply too much for a couple to take on for one day themselves and there's no way you'll be able to be fully present on your wedding day. While it's incredibly important to stick to your budget, you should also put a price on your sanity and wedding day chaos.

Mother Nature Is Not Your BFF

My number one piece of advice when looking for a venue if you want to have an outdoor ceremony and/or reception is to make sure that you love Plan B. Like *really* love it. Don't just settle for it because you have high hopes and the whole church praying for the perfect, sunny, 72 degree day. Weddings don't always move indoors just due to rain. Sometimes it is because it's too cold, too hot, too windy or too buggy. And let's get this out of the way right now. The one thing that we *cannot* control on your wedding day is Mother Nature. She has a serious attitude and there's nothing that we can do to stop it. I have had more couples cry over the weather than I would like to remember, so set the expectation right now that we have no idea where the ceremony will be until the week of the wedding and, no matter what, you love Plan A *and* Plan B.

The Logistics Nobody Talks About

No one warns you that weddings are less about magic and more about moving parts - literal, logistical moving parts. While everyone is busy debating napkin colors, someone still needs to unlock the doors, cue the music, line up the wedding party, feed the vendors and figure out where the gift and cards go so they don't accidentally take a ride home with Aunt Linda. Logistics are the unglamorous backbone of your wedding day, quietly ensuring that chairs appear before people sit and that you walk down the aisle to music instead of awkward silence. When you plan for the things no one posts about - timelines, transitions, backups and who's in charge when something goes sideways - you give yourself the ultimate luxury: a wedding day where you're not solving problems, working miracles and you're actually getting married.

Either during your tours or right after, ask the questions that nobody talks about but things that could really affect so many aspects of the day like your sanity, your guest's experience and your photos just to name a few.

Here are a few helpful and sanity-saving questions to ask that you might not be thinking about quite yet.

Do I Need to Plan for This?

1. Are all the spaces for the ceremony, cocktail hour and reception accessible for elderly guests? If not, do they provide accommodations such as a golf cart? Gram might not be into walking 3 miles uphill to your ceremony site.

2. Where is the parking and, if you hire transportation for your guests, where can they drop off/pick up your guests?

3. What lighting does your venue have where you will be taking photos and can it be controlled (dimmed or brightened)?

4. Are there any vendor restrictions or required vendors?

5. How many bathrooms are there and where are they located?

6. Who is in charge of the trash removal from the venue? (this is my *least* favorite subject, but it's one you'll want to know now and not have to figure out the night of your wedding after a few cocktails.)

7. Is this venue temperature controlled? If the venue manager uses the word 'rustic', this might be code for no heat or AC. (Think about everyone who will be wearing a 3-piece suit or the ladies with their makeup they don't want to melt off their faces.)

WARNING: I do not recommend touring more than 5 venues. After the fourth or fifth venue tour you will start to feel fatigued, suddenly your fiancé's sense of humor is no longer hilarious, and you can't even decide what you want to have for dinner that night let alone which venue you want to say "I do" in. Take a deep breath and step away. If you need to take a week or two away from talking about the big day or searching countless websites for the perfect venue, then do it. Wedding planning is a marathon, not a sprint. Pace yourself and give yourself time to make important decisions so that you don't regret them later.

With all of this said, it is possible that you may be the rare species that walks into their very first venue tour and says *"this is the one!"* In that case, pop the bubbles and pat yourself on the back, but don't be *that person* and brag about this to your other engaged friends who are now questioning every single detail of their wedding, are in full panic mode and scrolling Instagram at 2:00am to find their perfect venue.

What Can't You Live Without

Make a list of your non-negotiables – the things that you absolutely can't live without. Is it an indoor and outdoor option, the photo opportunities, getting ready suites onsite or maybe that you're allowed to use your own vendors? Make a list and check it twice. There will be venues that you fall in love with that are missing something from your list. Only you can decide if you can live with your venue missing that one thing (you have to use their caterer) or if you want to continue to research and tour venues. Just be sure that your expectations are realistic and you're not asking venues to include table, chairs and miracles.

Gut Check

At some point, you'll walk into a venue and just *feel* it. You'll stop making mental spreadsheets and start picturing yourself walking down the aisle. That's your cue. The perfect venue isn't about perfection; it's about how it fits *you*. The right place makes the planning feel easier, not harder. So yes, visit the barns, the ballrooms and the beaches. Take your Pinterest board with you, but let your gut make the final call. Because your heart knows what looks good on you.

When you're touring venues and making decisions, logic matters but your gut deserves a seat at the table (preferably with a cocktail). If a place looks perfect on paper but makes your shoulders tense or your stomach drop when the Venue Manager says "that's an extra fee," listen to that feeling. Your gut check is often the fastest way to separate what's impressive from what's right. The same goes for decisions: if you find yourself explaining, justifying or hoping something will magically feel better later, that's your intuition waving a tiny red flag. Trust it. The right venue and the right choices won't require mental gymnastics. They will bring a sense of calm, clarity and the quiet confidence of knowing you're building a day that actually fits you, not just photographs well.

CHAPTER 6

Vendors

Hiring the Dream Team

Your wedding vendors are basically super heros with special powers, each critical to saving your day. But unlike actual superheroes, these people are working for *you*, and you get to choose who makes up your dream team. The right vendors make your wedding planning feel effortless. The wrong ones make you consider eloping in the woods with nothing but a Bluetooth speaker and a cupcake.

You might have a board filled with 137 centerpieces (but please really try not to), 25 bouquets and a wedding cake shaped like a peony that defies gravity, but your vendors know how to execute those things without tears, burns, or broken relationships. A seasoned vendor has seen everything: late relatives, wilted flowers, heatwaves, hurricanes, groomsmen who ran off or got drunk, and DJs who accidentally played "WAP" during dinner. They know how to pivot with grace, and you want the team working for you to be one that has been in the trenches. Could you learn how to arrange florals, set up tables, coordinate timelines, run sound equipment, light candles, cue music, wrangle your wedding party, and manage transportation? Sure. It's not impossible. But should you? Absolutely not. Hiring qualified vendors buys you the right to be fully present on your wedding day. It's outsourcing stress and paying for peace of mind.

If wedding planning had a cast of characters, your vendors would be the ensemble that makes the whole show possible: the florist who speaks fluent peony, the photographer who can spot a perfect lighting moment at 50 paces and the wedding planner who can read a room better than most therapists. They are the people who turn your Pinterest board into something that doesn't burst into flames under real-world conditions.

But here's the plot twist that no one tells you: you do not need to become an expert in every vendor's job to hire them. In fact, please don't. You have enough on your plate, like remembering to drink water and pretending you understand the difference between ivory and eggshell.

Know What You Need (and What You Don't)

Before you start booking anyone, list the services that matter most to your vision and budget. For some couples, that's a killer live band. For others, it's a photographer who makes you look like you stepped out of a magazine. Skip the "must-have" list that wedding blogs push if it doesn't fit your *why* (refer to Chapter 1). You don't need thirteen vendors just because someone said you do. You need vendors that align with your vision, your budget, that give you and your guests a great experience and take care of the details that you can't…or don't want to. For example, if you don't want to manage the music, hire a DJ or band. If you don't want to make your own centerpieces and bouquets, hire a florist. If lighting and drapery isn't important to you, you might not need to hire a professional decorator. But keep in mind that you don't want to DIY everything (unless you secretly hate yourself).

Hiring vendors doesn't require a PHD in florals, lighting or sound engineering. It requires knowing what actually matters and letting go of the rest. You don't need to understand lens types to hire a great photographer, or the difference between peonies and ranunculus to trust a florist who gets your vision. What you *do* need to know is how a vendor communicates, whether they respect your budget and if they make you feel calm instead of confused. Great vendors aren't just talented, they're translators, problem solvers and professionals who know what you don't so you don't have to. When you hire people you trust, you stop micromanaging and start enjoying the process - which coincidentally, is the whole point.

The Interview Process

Think of hiring a vendor like dating. You're looking for chemistry, personality matches, and reliability. It's incredibly important that you feel confident in who you hire and that you enjoy their personality. It's a relationship. You're trusting them with milestones, moments, your money and your mother's opinion. If you don't vibe with them on the phone, you won't vibe with them when they're in your face on wedding day. You're not hiring robots. You're hiring humans who will be up close and personal on one of the most emotional days of your life.

You do not need to know how they created their work, just that they *did* and that you like it. When researching for your photographer look for full galleries, not just highlight reels where everyone looks like they walked straight off a skincare commercial. When researching for your florist look for weddings that feel similar to yours in scale and vibe. When researching for your caterer look for food that makes you involuntarily whisper "oh hell yes."

Important Questions to Ask Potential Vendors

"What's your backup plan if there's an emergency and you can't be there?"

Life happens. Illness happens. Weather happens. You are not being dramatic; you are being responsible. Listen for:

- A clear contingency plan
- Named backup professionals (not a vague "we'll figure it out")
- Contract language that explains substitutions

A professional vendor should answer this calmly and confidently.

"What is your communication style?"

Then make sure it actually works for you. Are They:

- Email-only?
- Text-friendly?
- Available during business hours only?
- Slow but thorough?
- Quick but brief?

If you are someone who needs reassurance and they respond once every 10 days, that mismatch will create unnecessary stress.

You are not "high maintenance." You just need clarity.

"Can you Work Within our Budget without Cutting Corners?"

You're not asking them to discount their value. You're asking them whether they can scale creatively and realistically. Great vendors know how to:

- Adjust scope
- Suggest alternatives
- Preserve quality while modifying quantity

If the only option is "upgrade or not", they might not be the right fit.

"Do you have business insurance?"

This one feels unromantic. Ask it anyway. Insurance protects:

- You
- The Venue
- The Vendor
- Everyone else.

Professional vendors expect this question. If they hesitate or don't have coverage, that is important information. (Your venue likely requires insurance as well)

Pay attention to their answers, but also to how they make you feel. If you leave the conversation more stressed than before, that's a sign. Also, take the time to read recent reviews. Reviews are incredibly insightful! A good vendor is proud of their experience and transparent with their track record. If you find any red flags (more in the next chapter) remember this is a business transaction, not a Hinge date.

Spotting Red Flags

When hiring your vendors, keep your eyes peeled for red flags because while your decor should be blush, your vendors' behavior absolutely should not be. If a vendor takes three to five business days (which feel like years) to reply, dodges direct questions or hands you a contract that reads like it was drafted by a raccoon with a fountain pen, proceed with caution. Trust your instincts. If something feels off, it probably is. And if their vibe gives you "I might ghost you two weeks before the wedding to pursue my dream as a travel influencer," RUN. A great vendor makes you feel informed, supported and safe, not confused, brushed off or like you need to open a bottle of wine just to decode their emails. Your wedding day should sparkle; your red flags shouldn't.

Spotting red flags when hiring your vendors is less about paranoia and more about paying attention to how your feel during the process. If someone is slow to respond, vague about pricing, dismissive of your budget or allergic to contracts, believe them the first time. A vendor who makes you feel rushed, confused or subtly shamed for asking questions is not setting the tone for a calm wedding day. The right professionals will welcome clarity, explain things without being condescending, and make you feel supported, not sold to. Planning a wedding is emotional enough, you don't need to ignore your instincts in the name of being "easy." Red flags don't get better with time. They just get more expensive.

Here a few more examples of things to look out for:

RED FLAG **Vague Pricing**

If they "can't" give you a clear price, they might be hiding fees.

RED FLAG **Slow Communication**

If they take three weeks to respond before you sign their contract, it won't get better after you book them.

RED FLAG **Overpromising**

We can absolutely do anything!" sounds great until they absolutely can't.

RED FLAG **Pushy Upsells**

Suggesting better options is fine, making you feel like your wedding is going to be sad unless you upgrade your package is not ok.

The Contract Is Your BFF

Vendor contracts may not be romantic and served with a glass of champagne and a warm hug, but they are wildly devoted to your peace of mind. Think of them as the prenup of wedding planning - clear, protective and designed to prevent awkward conversations later. A good contract spells out what's included, what's not, when money is due and what happens if plans change or the weather has a tantrum. It keeps expectations aligned and emotions out of negotiations, so you're not arguing over vague promises made during a giddy email exchange. When you read, understand and respect your contracts you're not being difficult, you're being intentional. Because nothing says "stress-free wedding" quite like everything being in writing.

If you are considering hiring a friend as a vendor, guess what? You still need a contract. Hiring your friends to work your wedding can feel like a win-win. You're supporting a small business, saving a little money and keeping it "in the family." And sometimes it is. But mixing friendship with responsibility without clear boundaries is a fast track to awkward feelings and unpaid emotional labor. If your friend is truly showing up as a vendor, treat them like one. Define the boundaries, the timeline, the pay and again, put it in a contract. A contract doesn't mean you don't trust them. It means that you value the friendship enough to protect it. Clear expectations keep resentment off the guest list and ensure your friend can celebrate with you *after* the job is done…ideally with a drink in hand, not a to-do list.

Build The Vibe

Your wedding vibe isn't created by a color palette alone. It's built by the people you hire to bring the day to life. Vendors set the tone long before the first song plays or the first drink is poured, which is why how they *feel* matters just as much as what they do. When you choose vendors who understand your vision, respect your boundaries and communicate with ease, the entire experience feels lighter, calmer and more you. The right team will protect your energy, not drain it, and somehow make even complicated logistics feel manageable. When your vendors are aligned with your vibe, your wedding doesn't just look good, it *feels* good. And that's what guests remember long after the cake is gone and the bar is closed.

You'll be spending a lot of time with some of your vendors on your wedding day (looking at you and maybe even up the back of your dress when it's time to bustle). Pick personalities that mesh with yours. If you want a calm, laid-back morning, don't book a photographer who thrives on shouting "BIG ENERGY!" every two minutes. If you love a hype squad, find people who can bring it. Your vendors aren't just service providers, they're the people helping you tell the story of your wedding day. Choose wisely, protect yourself with contracts and trust your gut. If something feels off now, it'll *really* feel off when you're wearing formalwear and trying to not sweat through it.

CHAPTER 7

Décor & Details That Actually Matter

Wedding decor is not about impressing Pinterest or proving you know the difference between champagne and ivory (spoiler: no one remembers). The details that actually matter are the ones your guests *experience,* not the ones they politely ignore while looking for the bar. Thoughtful lighting that makes people look alive, comfortable seating that doesn't feel like a folding chair punishment, signage that answers questions before Aunt Suzie asks them out loud - these are the unsung heroes. When decor supports the flow of the day, reflects who you are and makes people feel welcomed rather than overwhelmed it stops being "stuff" and starts being atmosphere. And atmosphere, unlike personalized favors with your wedding date, is something people actually take home with them.

Here's a truth the wedding industry doesn't always admit: you don't need everything. You don't need a donut wall and a champagne tower *and* custom monogrammed cocktail stirrers (unless that's your thing, in which case, you do you). You just need the right details – the ones that reflect *you* and make your guests feel the love. Put *your* heartbeat on your most special day. The rest? It's optional.

There's a difference between decor and details, and it's not the price tag. Decor is what people see. Details are what they feel. Flowers are lovely, but knowing where to sit, having a place to set down a drink and being able to hear the vows matter more. The details that count are the ones that make your guests feel considered like a timeline that actually makes sense, food that arrives when people are hungry and small personal touches that say "this is us." When you focus on details that create comfort, clarity and connection the decor stops needing to work so hard. Beauty fades, but a well thought out experience is what people remember long after the last centerpiece is cleared.

The "Does This Matter?" Test

When it comes to decor and details, every decision should pass one simple test: *does this actually matter?* Not to Instagram, not to your college roommate, not to the version of you who panic-scrolled at 1:00am, but to the experience you and your guests will have on the day. Will it make people more comfortable, more connected or more present? Or will it be admired for five seconds before being forgotten forever? If a detail reduces stress, adds meaning or improves the flow of the celebration, it passes. If it only adds cost, complexity or a mild emotional breakdown, it doesn't. The "does it matter" test isn't about cutting corners. It's about protecting what truly deserves your time, energy and champagne.

Before you add something to your décor list, ask:

1. Does this serve our "why" from Chapter 1?
2. Will anyone remember this in a year?
3. Will it make *us* happy on the day?

If the answer to all three is "yes," it stays. If it's more of a "meh" or "I just saw it on TikTok" let it go.

Choose a Vibe, Not a Theme

Themes can be really fun, but they can also get…intense. You don't want to be hunting down a very specific shade of mauve ribbon three weeks before the wedding because your "woodland vintage" theme demands it. Instead pick a vibe (think romantic, modern, cozy, bold) and choose colors, textures and lighting that match. That way you have freedom to adjust without the décor police (aka your own brain) issuing fines.

Themes tend to demand commitment, costumes and questionable decor choices. Vibes simply set the mood and let everything else fall into place. A vibe is how you want the day to *feel*: relaxed, romantic, joyful, wildly fun, deeply meaningful. When you choose a vibe instead of a theme, every decision gets easier from the music, lighting, florals and even the timeline because you're asking "does this fit the feeling?" not "does this match the concept?" A strong vibe gives your wedding cohesion without turning it into a production and it leaves room for personality, flexibility and real moments. Which conveniently, are always in style.

The Big Impact Items

If you want your wedding to feel elevated without losing your mind (or your budget), focus on big impact items. These are the choices guests actually notice such as the music that sets the energy, the lighting that transforms a space, the food and drinks that keep everyone happy and a few statement moments that make the day feel unmistakably yours. Big impact items don't need to be everywhere. They need to be *felt.* One great band beats ten small details and a beautifully timed moment will outshine a hundred tiny decor choices. When you invest where it counts, the rest of the day doesn't have to shout. It can simply glow.

If you want your décor to wow your guests without being overwhelming, focus on three high-impact elements such as the lighting, florals or a statement piece. For example, if you choose to focus on the lighting whether it's candles, string lights or uplighting. They change everything. If you want to focus on florals or greenery it doesn't have to be huge, but it should be intentional. If you want to focus on a statement piece such as an arbor, a dramatic table runner or a unique escort card display, make it something guests will remember. Everything else can be kept simple. Please read that sentence again.

When DIY is Worth It (and When It's Not)

DIY is great for personal touches, but dangerous when you're trying to recreate a professional floral chandelier or bouquets in your living room the night before your wedding. DIY is the glitter aisle of wedding planning: wildly tempting, occasionally magical and somehow ends up everywhere when you least expect it. When it's worth it, DIY can be deeply personal and budget-friendly. Think welcome bags, favors or anything you'd happily craft on a random Tuesday night with a glass of wine and zero pressure. When it's not worth it, DIY turns into a full-time job you never applied for, complete with deadlines, stress acne and a glue gun burn you'll still have in your photos. The rule of thumb is simple: if the project requires special skills, expensive tools or your emotional stability the week of your wedding, outsource it without guilt. Your time, sanity and ability to actually enjoy your wedding are far more valuable than the fact that you *could* have made the centerpieces yourself.

DIY wins are the projects that make you feel like a show-off in the best way - cute, affordable and finished *before* the week of the wedding. They photograph well, don't fall apart when touched by a gentle breeze and still spark joy after you've cleaned glitter out of your car. DIY fails on the other hand are the ones that seemed "easy enough" on Pinterest and now require a crisis meeting, three emergency trips to Target and a suspicious amount of hot glue. The difference is never ambition, it's timing, skill and realism. A true DIY win adds meaning without chaos. A DIY fail becomes a cautionary tale you'll tell future engaged friends while gently insisting they just hire someone.

DIY Wins

- Table Numbers.
- Signage.
- Sentimental details.
- Favors you can prep weeks in advance.
- Something that fits your actual skill set in real life.

DIY Fails

- Anything requiring refrigeration.
- Anything involving ladders or 3:00am assembly.
- Anything that makes you cry more than it makes you smile.

The Personal Touch

The details guests remember most are the ones that feel like *you*: A table named after the places you traveled to. A signature cocktail named after your pet. A ceremony reading from a favorite poem or song lyric.

At the end of the day, the goal of decor isn't to impress strangers on Instagram. It's to serve the people that love and support you in the room. When your details create comfort, guide the flow and quietly tell your story, they've done their job. If a choice brings you peace, makes your guests feel cared for or helps the day unfold with ease, it matters. If it only photographs well and keeps you up at night assembling it, let it go. The most beautiful weddings aren't defined by what was on the tables, but by how it all felt. Personal touches don't usually cost much, but they leave the deepest impression. And that's a detail worth investing in.

CHAPTER 8

The Emotional Wedding Roller Coaster

When you're engaged, you expect the guest's joy, love and maybe a little stress mixed with some opinions. What you *don't* expect is the full emotional marching band showing up with drums and questionable dance moves. Wedding planning isn't just a logistical project – it's an emotional roller coaster with no seatbelts or free snacks.

Wedding planning is less of a straight line and more of a theme park ride you didn't realize was included with your engagement ring. One minute you're floating on a cloud because you picked napkins you love and the next you're spiraling because someone used the phrase "family expectations." The emotional whiplash is normal, unavoidable and not a sign that you're doing anything wrong. It's simply what happens when your joy, money, memories and opinions all share the same group chat. The goal isn't to stay calm at all times (impossible), but to remember that every high and low is temporary. Breathe, hydrate and trust that the moment you walk down the aisle the roller coaster slows, the noise fades and the only thing left is the reason you got on the ride in the first place.

Wedding planning is sold as a highlight reel but lived as a full-contact emotional sport. One minute you're floating on cloud nine because you found the perfect dress, and the next you're crying in your car because you're stressing out over napkin colors (true story). Joy, stress, excitement, grief and the sudden urge to text your fiancé "I'M GOING TO LOSE IT!" will rotate through your body with alarming speed. This is normal. You are not dramatic; you are planning a major life transition while coordinating logistics usually reserved for corporate retreats and presidential state dinners. Emotions come and go, and it's important to slow down, recognize them, and find your way through the moment.

Let's meet the usual suspects…

EMOTION: *Blissful Excitement*

This is the ***"I'm getting MARRIED!"*** high where everything feels magical. You love every flower you see. You cry at proposal videos of strangers you see on Instagram. You start signing emails "The Future Mrs./Mr." even to your dentist.

Write down this feeling in the notes app on your phone. You'll need it later when you're in centerpiece decision fatigue.

EMOTION: ***Overwhelmed***

At some point, you'll realize your to-do list is breeding more to-do lists. You'll wake up in the night wondering if you remembered to confirm the coffee and dessert station. Your browser tabs will include "ivory vs cream linens" and "how to politely uninvite someone."

Break it into small pieces. Treat wedding tasks like Netflix episodes and do one or two at a time, not the whole season in one night.

EMOTION: ***The "What If" Panic***

"What if it rains?"
"What if the DJ plays the wrong first-dance song?"
"What if Aunt Suzie wears that shirt again?"
"What if the seating chart gets hijacked by plus ones?"

REALITY CHECK:

Something probably will go sideways. It will not ruin your wedding. In fact, it will likely become one of your favorite "remember when?" stories.

EMOTION: ***Family Drama Queen***

Ahh yes, the moment you realize that weddings are also family-reunions. People you haven't spoken to in five years suddenly have strong opinions on your centerpieces.

Use the magical phrase, "That's a great idea, we'll think about it." Which in Wedding-ese translates to, "That's never happening."

EMOTION: *Random Tearfulness*

You might cry over your vows…or because you can't find the right shade of olive green. Both are valid.

Take a deep breath and let it out. Keep tissues in your wedding binder (and in your purse, glove compartment and bra).

EMOTION: *Pure Joy*

In the middle of the chaos, you'll have flashes of "this is exactly right." It might be during a cake tasting or when you see your partner smile at you across the room while discussing the floor layout. These moments are the soul of your wedding.

Remember these moments when things feel tough. Savor it and drink it in.

EMOTION: *Post- Wedding "Now What?"*

No one talks about the quiet after the big day. Suddenly, your evenings are wide open and no one is texting you about chicken vs. beef or the hotel room block. It can feel…weird.

Plan a little post-wedding something – print photos, host a game night or start a "Tuesday Date Night" tradition. Love is a lifetime project, not just a one-day event.

Stop trying to get off the roller coaster. You bought the ticket the moment you said "yes" and pretending you're above the emotions only guarantees a dramatic mid-ride meltdown. Wedding planning compresses excitement, pressure, family dynamics, money, memories and expectations into one sparkly timeline…and your nervous system notices. The goal isn't emotional perfection, it's emotional awareness. When you name what you're feeling instead of fighting it, the ride immediately gets less jerky (and far less likely to end in tears at Target).

Build in emotional pit stops. You cannot white-knuckle your way through this season and expect to arrive glowing. Step away from Pinterest. Schedule check-ins with your partner that have nothing to do with place cards or timelines. Eat real meals. Go outside. Touch grass. The most effective coping strategy during wedding planning is remembering that you are a human being first and a bride second. When everything starts to feel overwhelming, it's usually not a sign to push hard, it's a sign to pause.

Zoom out when the feelings get loud. Ask yourself: will this matter in five years? Five months? Five minutes after the bar opens? Most emotional spikes are not about the wedding itself, but about the meaning we attach to it. Anchor yourself to the marriage you're building, not the moment you're managing. This season is temporary, the emotions are valid and the love is real. Ride the highs, survive the lows and trust that you don't need to control every turn to enjoy the ride. Just hold on, breathe deep and keep moving forward together.

Here's the sneaky part about this emotional roller coaster: the emotions rarely match the moment. You might lose it over a seating chart when what you're really feeling is pressure, family expectations, or the quiet realization that life is changing forever. Weddings stir up *everything*, past relationships, absent loved ones, financial stress and the weight of wanting this day to mean something. Let the feelings come without assuming they're a sign that you're doing it wrong. Sometimes tears are just your nervous system asking for a snack and a nap.

The key to surviving wedding planning isn't avoiding the highs and lows. It's refusing to make permanent decisions while strapped in a temporary spiral. Breathe. Pause. Zoom out. This season is intense because it matters, not because it's broken. Keep your eye on the marriage, not the momentary meltdown and remember, no one ever looks back on their wedding and says "if only I had been more stressed." Ride the waves, hold your partner's hand and trust that on the other side of this whirlwind is a day, and a life, worth feeling.

If the emotional wedding roller coaster taught you anything, it's that you are far more resilient than you realized and that seating charts can, in fact, make grown adults cry. You felt the highs, survived the lows and learned that joy and stress can coexist without canceling each other out. When the day finally arrives, the details fade, the opinions quiet and the ride gently comes to a stop. What remains isn't the anxiety, the second guessing or the moments you almost lost it over font choices (I personally have lost it over font choices). It's the love that made every loop and drop worth it. And if nothing else, you walk away with a great marriage and an excellent story about how you lived to tell the tale.

CHAPTER 9

Wedding Day Regrets

(The Things You Wish You Didn't Care So Much About)

The Myth of No Regrets

Everyone says they have no regrets. They're lying. Or they've blocked it out like childbirth. The truth is, almost every couple walks away from their wedding with a tiny list of things they'd tweak if they had to do it again – from skipping the 40-minute sunset photos you rushed to take instead of eating dinner, or the 5-tiered cake that looked gorgeous, but no one ate. Most regrets come from either trying to squeeze too much into one day or forgetting to be fully present.

Common Wedding Regrets

Overspending for show instead of for meaning is first on the list. Your guests won't remember the monogrammed cocktail napkins or the flowers on the arbor. They will remember if there was an open bar and whether your DJ kept everyone on the dance floor. They will throw away their place card unless it is something meaningful. One of my favorite place cards were small white frames with black and white photos of the guests. I still have it on my dresser, and the couple celebrated their 14th anniversary last summer. Money buys a lot of things, but it can't buy good vibes, meaningful touches, and awesome dance-floor moves. Spend your time, energy and money on things that are important to you. Things that tell your love story, enhance the overall experience and vibe of the big day. You won't look back and say 'I wish I spent more money on the favors that no one took.' Instead, you might be grateful for feeding the wedding party brunch and mimosas while getting ready and having that time together in the morning. You won't look back and say 'I wish I spent more money on the card box that I'll only use once.' Instead, you might be grateful for the photo booth that captured everyone having a great time.

Delegate and Plan, Plan, Plan

You have been a multi-tasking, emailing, phone call and vendor meeting machine for months now. On wedding day, it's time to hand over the reins. I don't suggest handing them over to Aunt Suzie who will be drunk by 8:00pm, but perhaps a wedding planner or a sober and super responsible family member (one that you don't mind if they have a job and don't really feel like a guest). Delegate every single task that another human being can take care of for you. Don't try to be a hero and think that you will have time to set up the ceremony arbor and centerpieces before you have to be in the makeup chair. You want to enjoy that time with your wedding party, getting ready, sipping champagne and dancing to your favorite 'let's get married' songs while taking photos in your matching PJs. Delegate someone to bring you and the wedding party brunch, lunch, snacks, drinks and water…lots of water. Moms often love this job. It gives them a task to keep them busy in the morning, not pacing the reception venue wondering when the linens will be there, and it makes them feel important.

Plan which shoes you are going to wear to walk down the aisle without limping, and which shoes you're going to do your first dance in without stepping on your dress. Plan who your designated lipstick and deodorant person will be. Plan what you and your spouse want to do when it's time to be introduced into your reception. Do you want to walk in carrying your bouquet or your signature cocktail?

And for the love of wine, don't forget to plan your exit at the end of the night. If your vision is to have a private last dance, a send-off and leave the venue on cloud nine…then plan it. Where do you go when you exit? Who is in charge of your bridal bag in the suite and your veil? If you want an Irish goodbye, then have the DJ announce the last song so you know it's your cue to quietly and discreetly exit to your after party. If your vision is to stay until the very end of the night and say goodbye to every single one of your guests…just know that I warned you. Clean up after a wedding happens abruptly and quickly because your venue and vendor team need to honor your contracted time and they have an hour to clean up…and they just worked a 14-hour day and want to go home. Think long and hard about the very last note you want to leave your wedding on and the feeling that you want to leave with as your headed to your after party or hotel. Delegate, and plan, plan, plan!

Missing The Moment for the Photos

You will spend more time smiling for the camera than smiling at your spouse and guests. Don't let your memories be of your photographer yelling "one more shot!" while your dinner gets cold or you miss the chance to say goodbye to Gram before she leaves after dinner because it's her bedtime. If the cake cutting photo isn't important to you then skip it. I strongly suggest building in quiet moments into your timeline. Moments where you two can breathe, be together and connect with each other. It's your wedding day! Don't you want to know how your newly married spouse is feeling?! If not, maybe wedding planning really did get the best of you. In this case, I hope you can reconnect and have quiet moments together on your mini-moon or honeymoon or we have bigger problems.

Not Eating, Drinking or Sitting Down

As a Wedding Planner I am always trying to feed my couples and give them moments to breathe, but you would be surprised how many couples have survived their wedding day on adrenaline, one piece of shrimp cocktail and forkful of wedding cake. Just like building in quiet moments together, build in time to eat and make it a priority. Call it "mandatory feeding time." It's a thing now.

You might be able to live off one shrimp for a day, but the next morning it will only make the "event hangover" a million times worse. Yes, the event hangover is a very real-life thing. It's when your body crashes hard after all the planning, excitement, emotions, adrenaline and lack of sleep. It usually hits you the morning after the wedding and you'll know because you will feel like you were side swiped by a mac truck, topped it with 4 glasses of champagne and very little sleep. The absolute best way to avoid this is to sit down, be present, eat the food that you took weeks to decide on and sip the signature cocktails that you so carefully chose. Don't forget to hydrate with water and electrolytes like your life depends on it. This is wedding day self-care and it should be a priority.

I Should've Worn the Comfy Shoes

Yes, the expensive designer shoes are stunning and will look amazing in photos, but they are a slow torture device covered in sparkles. The saying "beauty is pain" should not be said on one of the most special days of your life. Think of your wedding day as a marathon, not a sprint…one that you need comfortable shoes on your feet for 12 hours. Waking up the morning after your wedding with blisters, sore feet or dirty feet because you completely ditched the shoes doesn't win you the "bride of the year" award. There's no such thing. On wedding day comfort always wins and keeps you smiling all night long, instead of grimacing because your blister is growing with every dance move you make.

I've watched brides go into their wedding day bag, pull out the lidocaine spray, tear their heels off like their bra at the end of a long week and spray their feet like their life depends on it with tears of regret in their eyes. It's simply just not worth it.

Micromanaging the Seating Chart

Remember the guest list we talked in Chapter 2? Do you remember me saying it's the 'most emotional spreadsheet you will ever create?' Well, then came the sleepless nights over the seating chart. Stop. Right. Now. Aunt Suzie and Cousin Becky survived sitting 3 chairs away from each other. No one combusted.

When you start looking at your guest list and piecing the puzzle together and deciding who gets along, who knows each other and who wants to be closest to the dance floor. Remind yourself that they will most likely be in their seat for a total of 60 minutes for dinner. That's 60 minutes out of your 300-minute reception. After they have a conversation with their "table buddies" and eat their dinner - they will head back to the bar, the dance floor or over to another table to continue having conversations. Everyone will live and more importantly, they will have a great time celebrating you.

I've been in more meetings, phone calls and emails than I like to talk about regarding the seating chart. It tends to be one of the most overthought pieces of wedding planning and conveniently enough, you can't start working on your seating chart until you start to receive RSVPs…3-4 weeks before the wedding when it's go time. Take a deep breath, keep an open mind and grab another cup of coffee (or bottle of wine). If your venue tables can seat up to 8 guests, that does not mean that you have to have 8 guests at the table. I suggest not doing less than 5 at a table or your guests might start to feel like they're at the "misfit table." Also, don't hesitate to ask your venue if they have other size tables. Most venues have options that can accommodate the smaller and larger groups that you "just can't separate."

Letting that One Thing Ruin 70 Gorgeous Things

Suddenly, one bouquet starts to wilt and panic sets in as you consider calling the florist. Don't let it ruin your day. The truth is none of your guests are looking at your bridesmaids bouquets (unless they are a florist for a living). They are looking at you and your new spouse.

Walk into your wedding day with the mentality that something *will* go wrong and it will be fine. I promise it will only be one moment in time, and you have a much better chance of keeping your sanity and enjoying your day with this mindset. No one but you (and maybe your wedding planner) knows every single detail that you have planned and lost sleep over. No one knows exactly how the DJ was supposed to let the song play during the processional before the wedding party walked down the aisle. No one knows that the flower girl and ring bearer were supposed to walk in separately and 5 seconds beforehand they had a full-blown meltdown, so they walked down together. Not only does no one know, but truthfully, no one cares. They are there to see you and your new spouse commit yourselves to each other and to celebrate with you. So, if something does go wrong, laugh it off and enjoy telling the stories for years to come.

I Should've Made a Must-Have Photo List

Realizing that your photographer took, edited and delivered 1,300 photos to you and there's 337 of your centerpieces and none of you and your grandmother is regret level MAX. Just like everything else on wedding day, this takes a little effort and planning out who you want photos with on your wedding day. The more detailed and specific, the better. Your opinionated Aunt Betty might not be your favorite person to have family dinner with, but will you regret not having a photo with her? Perhaps this is the first time that you and your college friends will all be together since the last football game and you want a photo? Make a list of all their names and plan when you want this photo to take place. If you don't, you won't get the photo.

When it comes to pictures there are 2 types of brides: The one who wants photos of everything and everyone, or the bride who says *"photos aren't as important as being on the dance floor"*. No matter which bride you are, you still need to make the photo list so that you get all of the photos that you want and don't waste time getting them. You also don't want to waste time having to chase down Uncle Joey in the cocktail hour for that one photo, so let everyone that you want in photos know ahead of time. It is taking the extra step to let them know when and where you want them to meet you for photos (such as the alter after the ceremony) but it will help keep you sane and get you to your party sooner.

Forgetting the Purpose

It's your wedding and your marriage, not a Broadway show. You're not performing love, you're beginning it. It's human and easy to get caught up in the details and the decisions because there are so many of them. Did the napkins get folded the way I wanted? Did the candles get lit on time? Will the DJ play the right song when I walk down the aisle? What is the weather? It's a lot…if you let it be. Or you can keep reminding yourself what is actually about to take place.

You are about to marry your person, your best friend and spend the rest of your life with them. You are about to celebrate your love in a room full of all of the people who love and support you. It's pretty rare that after the wedding day you will have all of those people together again under the same roof at the same time. Soak up that time with them! Take a step back, look at the room full of your people, look at your spouse and remember the whole purpose of your wedding day.

CHAPTER 10

And They Lived Happily (and Sanely) Ever After

This is the part where you remember why you did all of this. Here you are. You survived wedding planning – emotionally, financially and possibly still speaking to most of your family. Congratulations!

When you first started this journey, it was all ring selfies and Pinterest boards. Then came the guest list math, budget aerobics and in-depth Google search for "how to remove hot glue from your hair." Now? You're about to marry your person. And that's the sole purpose to all of this.

What You'll Actually Remember

Spoiler alert: It probably won't be whether the flowers were blush or dusty rose. You'll remember the moment you locked eyes with your partner during the ceremony, the way your friends laughed on the dance floor and that one relative who took "open bar" as a personal challenge and ended the night with his tie on his head.

After the wedding your memory will not preserve the exact shade of blush or whether the napkins were folded "correctly" no matter how many hours you spent debating them. What you will remember are the moments that slipped past the timeline. The way your hands shook just a little before the ceremony, the laugh you didn't expect during the vows, the song that pulled everyone onto the dance floor at the same time. You'll remember who showed up, who hugged you a beat longer and how it felt when the room exhaled and celebrated with you. The details mattered in the planning because they got you there, but the memories that last are the ones that couldn't be curated, ordered or pinned. Those are the things you'll carry long after the last candle is blown out.

The Myth of Perfection

Let's be real: perfection is overrated. Something will go a little sideways. It might be small (the flower girl refuses to walk down the aisle) or medium (the caterer forgets the bread rolls). But here's the plot twist: those little hiccups make the best stories later. Think of it this way. If everything went exactly as planned, your wedding recap would be about three sentences long. And where's the fun in that?

Somewhere between the engagement announcement and your third vendor meeting you will be introduced to the idea that your wedding can be perfect. Not meaningful. Not joyful. Not deeply personal. Perfect. This myth is aggressively marketed, beautifully photographed and almost entirely fictional. It whispers that if you choose the right venue, the right color palette and the right font pairing, everything will fall into place and you will float through your wedding day like a calm, glowing goddess with excellent posture.

Let's be clear - perfection is not a wedding goal, it's a trap. It suggests that there is one correct way to do this and that deviation equals failure. It turns tiny, harmless details into moral dilemmas and convinces you that one wrong decision could somehow ruin a day that is literally about two people committing their lives to each other. That's a lot of pressure to put on napkins.

The truth is that weddings are live events, involving humans, emotions, weather and at least one person who didn't read the timeline that was so beautifully crafted. Something will go off script. A boutonniere will wilt. A song will start too early or too late. Someone will say something weird. None of this means your wedding isn't beautiful; it means it's real. And real is far more memorable than flawless.

Chasing perfection also steals your joy in advance. It keeps you focused on what might go wrong instead of what is already going right. It turns planning into a constant state of evaluation rather than anticipation. When perfection is the goal, nothing ever feels finished, good enough or worthy of celebration. And if there's one thing a wedding deserves, it's to be celebrated, not audited.

A meaningful wedding doesn't happen because every detail aligns, it happens because you are present for it. You notice the way your partner looks at you during the ceremony. You feel the room shift from nerves to relief to joy. You laugh when something unexpected happens because it reminds you that you're alive, in love and surrounded by people who love and support you. Those moments cannot be perfected, but they are deeply felt and last a lifetime

The Big Picture

After the last song plays, the cake is gone and your dance shoes are in the corner looking like survivors of a mild tornado, you'll realize something: the wedding was one incredible day. Marriage is the real adventure. Wedding planning teaches you things you'll use forever – like compromise, patience and the fine art of smiling politely while ignoring really bad advice. Those skills will come in handy when you're deciding on your first couch together or figuring out who's in charge of the dishes. Let's not even have the conversation "what do you want to eat for dinner tonight?"

If you take nothing else from this book, take this: a perfect wedding has never been the point. The flowers will wilt, the timeline will flex, and someone will forget where they parked, but the marriage is what lasts. Planning with intention means choosing meaning over perfection, people over optics, and joy over comparison. It doesn't matter whether everything went exactly as planned, the goal is to marry the right person and laugh at least once along the way.

The skills you practiced here - setting boundaries, communicating clearly, managing expectations and letting go of what doesn't matter - are not wedding skills. They are marriage skills. Long after the dress is boxed and the thank you notes are mailed, you'll still be choosing each other in small, ordinary moments. Turns out happily ever after isn't one big magical ending - it's a daily decision often made in sweatpants, sometimes over takeout and always rooted in love.

Final Toast

So step into your wedding day fully present. Eat the cake. Hold hands. Let the moment be imperfect and unforgettable. Then walk forward into your marriage knowing you planned this season with purpose, humor, and heart, and that intention will carry through whatever comes next. Here's to a love that grows, a partnership that lasts and a life together that's even better than the wedding. Happily ever after looks good on you. Now close this book, go marry your person, and start the rest of your life together.

Acknowledgments

If planning weddings for a living has taught me anything, it's that nothing meaningful happens alone; not a perfect timeline, not a seamless wedding day and certainly not this book.

To my extraordinary friend and publisher, Dr. Lara Paparo, my incredible Simple Soiree team, and my brilliant colleagues: thank you for being my sounding board, hype squad and voice of reason when I was almost one coffee away from burning the pages in this book rather than printing them. Your encouragement and support were a tremendous help through countless drafts, edits and moments of wondering why I started this personal project in the first place. You are the behind-the-scenes MVPs.

Thank you for cheering me on and for reminding me that intentional work, like weddings, is built on gut instincts, patience, determination and a little bit of humor when things get weird (because they always do). This book exists because of your support on this journey. I am endlessly grateful and I promise to always have a seat at my table for you.

With deep appreciation (and probably a clipboard), thank you.

-Kaci

www.ingramcontent.com/pod-product-compliance
Lightning Source LLC
LaVergne TN
LVHW020658100826
845148LV00012B/2555